In case of loss, p

As a reward: _____

Voyageur

A TRAVELLER'S NOTEBOOK
FOR THE DIGITAL AGE

You've done it. You've booked your flights, your camera's loaded, you've got your hands on this rather nice Voyageur notebook. You're ready to depart on your adventure.

This Voyageur notebook will be your indispensable travelling companion, faithfully recording your memories, holding your notes and sketches, containing your trip mementos. But there are also a few clever ways in which you can connect it to the digital world.

Visit moleskine.com/voyageur to access all the online tools available to augment your notebook and bring it into the world wide web. Check them all out below. And remember, planning your trip is part of the journey.

Download useful travel add-ons at:

moleskine.com/voyageur

name	surname
home address	
telephone	mobile
e-mail	website

company name	
business address	
telephone	mobile
e-mail	website

identity card no.	valid until
passport no.	valid until
visa	valid until
visa	valid until
credit card	valid until
driver's licence	valid until
car plate	motorcycle plate

family doctor	telephone
blood group	rhesus
allergies	
vaccination	valid until
vaccination	valid until
health insurance	valid until
travel insurance	valid until
contacts in emergency	

A TRAVELLER'S NOTEBOOK FOR THE DIGITAL AGE

Augment your *Voyageur* notebook experience
through the following tools:

BRING YOUR PRINT-OUTS TO YOUR NOTES

Avoid crumpled hotel bookings and lost email confirmations
by bringing them to your notebook. Enter any website URL
into the "Import Content" section and download the page in
Voyageur dimensions ready to print out and paste into your
notebook. No more loose sheets.

DOWNLOAD USEFUL ADD-ONS

Run out of the checklists in the back? Download some more and add them in.

moleskine.com/voyageur   print   paste

SNAP A SELFIE

Check the paper-band wrapped around the *Voyageur* notebook: the design o
the back makes the perfect photo prop. Post your B-side selfie on social and ta
it **#m_iamhere** to let us know you're on the road.

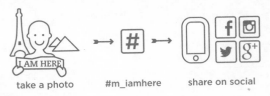

take a photo   #m_iamhere   share on social

MAP YOUR TRIP

Share your trip on the *Moleskine around the world* Flickr group and check in on the map to join fellow voyageurs around the world.

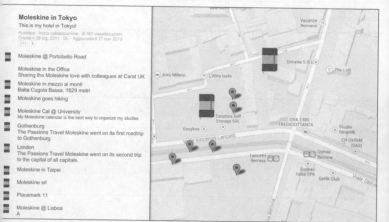

PRESERVE YOUR MEMORIES

Taken some good photos? Keep your trip memories alive for longer by printing them in a Moleskine Photo Book with this online tool.

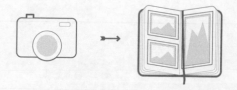

moleskine.com/voyageur

LOYALTY CARDS

card name

number

notes

card name

number

notes

card name

number

notes

card name

number

notes

card name

number

notes

card name

number

notes

card name

number

notes

card name

number

notes

card name

number

notes

card name

number

notes

card name

number

notes

card name

number

notes

Country	General Emergencies	Police	Medical	Fire
Afghanistan				
Albania		129	127 (a)	
Algeria		17 (b), 021735350 (c)	021236381 (c)	14 (b), 021711414 (c)
Andorra	112			
Angola		113	116	115
Antigua and Barbuda	911			
Argentina	911	911	107	100
Armenia	911	102	103	101
Australia	000			
Austria	112	133	144	122
Azerbaijan	112	102	103	101
Bahamas	911, 919			
Bahrain	999			
Bangladesh	02999, 999 (a)			02999, 999 (a)
Barbados		211	511	311
Belarus		102	103	101
Belgium	112	101	100	
Belize	911			
Benin		117		118
Bhutan		113	112	
Bolivia	110	110	118	119
Bosnia and Herzegovina		122	124	123
Botswana		999	997	998
Brazil		190	192	193
Brunei		993	998	995
Bulgaria	112	166	150	160
Burkina Faso	1010	17 (a), 50306383 (a)	50306644/5 (a)	18 (a), 50306947 (a)
Burundi		112 (a)		
Cambodia		117	119	118
Cameroon	3436572 (a)	17		18
Canada	911			
Cape Verde		132	130	131
Central African Rep.	117	21612200		
Chad		17	2527726	18
Chile		133	131	132
China	999 (d)	110	120	119
Colombia	123			
Comoros		17		
Congo	112, 066654804			
Congo, Dem. Rep.	199			
Costa Rica	911			
Côte d'Ivoire	111			
Croatia	112	192	112	193
Cuba	106	106	104	105
Cyprus	112 (e)			
Czech Republic	112	158	155	150
Denmark	112 (f)			
Djibouti		17		18
Dominica	999			

Country	General Emergencies	Police	Medical	Fire
Dominican Republic	911	6822151	5320000	
Ecuador	911 (a)	101	131	102
Egypt	122	123	180	
El Salvador	911			
Equatorial Guinea	113 (a)	114		115
Eritrea		114620 (a), 114942 (a)		
Estonia	112			
Ethiopia	991	911 (a)	902 (a), 907 (a)	902 (a), 903 (a)
Fiji		917	911	911
Finland	112			
France	112	17	15	18
Gabon		177	747474	18
Gambia		17, 117	16, 116	18, 118
Georgia	112			
Germany	112	110		
Ghana		191	193	192
Greece	112	100	166	199
Grenada	911	911	434	911
Guatemala		110, 120	125, 128	122, 123
Guinea		30471036 (g)		
Guinea-Bissau		117	113	118
Guyana	911	911	913	912
Haiti	114			
Honduras		199	195	198
Hungary	112	107	104	105
Iceland	112			
India	100 (b), 112 (c)			
Indonesia	112	110	118	113
Iran	110, 112 (c)	110	115	125
Iraq	130			
Ireland	112, 999			
Israel		100	101	102
Italy	112	113	118	115
Jamaica		119	110	110
Japan		110	119	119
Jordan	911			
Kazakhstan	112	102	103	101
Kenya	999			
Kiribati	999	992	994	993
Korea (North)				
Korea (South)		112	119, 129	119
Kuwait	112			
Kyrgyzstan		102	103	101
Laos		191	195	190
Latvia	112	110	113	
Lebanon		112	125, 140	175
Lesotho	112			
Liberia	911 (b), 355 (c)			
Libya	1515			
Liechtenstein	112	117	144	118
Lithuania	112	02		
Luxembourg	112	113		

When calling from a foreign mobile phone, all numbers must be preceded by the national dialling cod

Country	General Emergencies	Police	Medical	Fire
Macedonia		192	194	193
Madagascar	117			118
Malawi	997	997	998	999
Malaysia		999	999	994
Maldives	119	119	102	
Mali	17, 18	18	15	17
Malta	112	21224001/7, 21221111		
Marshall Islands	911, 1911			
Mauritania		17	5252135	18
Mauritius	999	112	114	
Mexico	066			
Micronesia	911			
Moldova	112	902	903	901
Monaco	112	17	18	18
Mongolia		102	103	101
Montenegro		122	124	123
Morocco		190, 177	150	
Mozambique	112, 119			
Myanmar		199	192	191
Namibia	112	10115	211111	
Nauru		110	111, 4443883	112
Nepal	100			
Netherlands	112			
New Zealand	111			
Nicaragua	118, 101 (h)			
Niger	17, 20722553 (a)			
Nigeria	199			
Norway	112	112	113	110
Oman	999			
Pakistan	15			
Palau	911			
Palestinian territories		100	101	102
Panama	911	104	911	103
Papua New Guinea	000			110
Paraguay	911			131, 132
Peru		105	115	116
Philippines	117			
Poland	112	997	999	998
Portugal	112			
Qatar	999			
Romania	112			
Russian Federation	112	02	02	001
Rwanda		112		
Saint Kitts and Nevis	911	4652241		
Saint Lucia	911			
Saint Vincent and the Grenadines	999			
Samoa		995	996	994
San Marino	113	115	118	115
Sao Tome and Principe	222222			112
Saudi Arabia		999 (a)	997 (a)	998 (a)

Country	General Emergencies	Police	Medical	Fire
Senegal	17	338237149		
Serbia		192	194	193
Seychelles	999			
Sierra Leone	999	15		
Singapore		999	995	995
Slovakia	112	158	155	
Slovenia	112	113		
Solomon Islands	999		911	988
Somalia	888			
South Africa		10111	10177	
South Sudan				
Spain	112	091	061	080
Sri Lanka		119	110	
Sudan	999 (a)			
Suriname	112	115	113	
Swaziland	999			
Sweden	112			
Switzerland		117	144	118
Syria		112	110	113
Taiwan	119	110	119	119
Tajikistan		02	03	01
Tanzania	111			
Thailand	191			199
Timor-Leste	112			
Togo		117 (b), 161 (c)		118
Tonga	911	922	933	
Trinidad and Tobago	999	999	990	990
Tunisia		197	190	198
Turkey	155	155	112	110
Turkmenistan		02	03	
Tuvalu	911			
Uganda	999			
Ukraine	112	102	103	101
United Arab Emirates	999	999	998	997
United Kingdom	112	999	999	
Uruguay	911	109	105	
Usa	911			
Uzbekistan		102	103	101
Vanuatu		112, 22222	112, 22100	112, 22333
Vatican City	66982			
Venezuela	171			
Vietnam		113	115	114
Yemen	199			
Zambia	999	991	991	993
Zimbabwe	999 (a)	995 (a)		994 (a)

only for the capital city   (b) from landline   (c) from mobile   (d) only for Hong Kong and Macau
all emergencies for the Northern zone dial 155 - dialling code 90392   (f) including Greenland
French Embassy Medical Centre   (h) English speaking service

DIALLING CODES, INTERNET TLD, PLATE CODES

Country	Dialling Code	Internet Tld	Plate Code
Afghanistan	93	.af	AFG
Albania	355	.al	AL
Algeria	213	.dz	DZ
Andorra	376	.ad	AND
Angola	244	.ao	ANG
Antigua/Barb.	1268	.ag	AG
Argentina	54	.ar	RA
Armenia	374	.am	AM
Australia	61	.au	AUS
Austria	43	.at	A
Azerbaijan	994	.az	AZ
Bahamas	1242	.bs	BS
Bahrain	973	.bh	BRN
Bangladesh	880	.bd	BD
Barbados	1246	.bb	BDS
Belarus	375	.by	BY
Belgium	32	.be	B
Belize	501	.bz	BH
Benin	229	.bj	DY
Bhutan	975	.bt	BHT
Bolivia	591	.bo	BOL
Bosnia/Herz.	387	.ba	BIH
Botswana	267	.bw	BW
Brazil	55	.br	BR
Brunei	673	.bn	BRU
Bulgaria	359	.bg	BG
Burkina Faso	226	.bf	BF
Burundi	257	.bi	RU
Cambodia	855	.kh	K
Cameroon	237	.cm	CAM
Canada	1	.ca	CDN
Cape Verde	238	.cv	CV
Centr. Afr. Rep.	236	.cf	RCA
Chad	235	.td	TCH
Chile	56	.cl	RCH
China	86	.cn	PRC
Colombia	57	.co	CO
Comoros	269	.km	COM
Congo	242	.cg	RCB
Congo, Dem. Rep.	243	.cd	ZRE
Costa Rica	506	.cr	CR
Côte d'Ivoire	225	.ci	CI
Croatia	385	.hr	HR
Cuba	53	.cu	C
Cyprus	357	.cy	CY
Czech Rep.	420	.cz	CZ
Denmark	45	.dk	DK
Djibouti	253	.dj	DJI
Dominica	1767	.dm	WD
Dominican Rep.	1809	.do	DOM

Country	Dialling Code	Internet Tld	Plate Code
Ecuador	593	.ec	EC
Egypt	20	.eg	ET
El Salvador	503	.sv	ES
Equat. Guinea	240	.gq	GQ
Eritrea	291	.er	ER
Estonia	372	.ee	EST
Ethiopia	251	.et	ETH
Fiji	679	.fj	FJI
Finland	358	.fi	FIN
France	33	.fr	F
Gabon	241	.ga	G
Gambia	220	.gm	WAG
Georgia	995	.ge	GE
Germany	49	.de	D
Ghana	233	.gh	GH
Greece	30	.gr	GR
Greenland	299	.gl	KN
Grenada	1473	.gd	WG
Guatemala	502	.gt	GCA
Guinea	224	.gn	RG
Guinea-Bissau	245	.gw	GNB
Guyana	592	.gy	GUY
Haiti	509	.ht	RH
Honduras	504	.hn	HN
Hong Kong	852	.hk	HK
Hungary	36	.hu	H
Iceland	354	.is	IS
India	91	.in	IND
Indonesia	62	.id	RI
Iran	98	.ir	IR
Iraq	964	.iq	IRQ
Ireland	353	.ie	IRL
Israel	972	.il	IL
Italy	39	.it	I
Jamaica	1876	.jm	JA
Japan	81	.jp	J
Jordan	962	.jo	HKJ
Kazakhstan	7	.kz	KZ
Kenya	254	.ke	EAK
Kiribati	686	.ki	KIR
Korea (North)	850	.kp	DVRK
Korea (South)	82	.kr	ROK
Kuwait	965	.kw	KWT
Kyrgyzstan	996	.kg	KS
Laos	856	.la	LAO
Latvia	371	.lv	LV
Lebanon	961	.lb	RL
Lesotho	266	.ls	LS
Liberia	231	.lr	LB
Libya	218	.ly	LAR

Country	Dialling Code	Internet Tld	Plate Code
Liechtenstein	423	.li	FL
Lithuania	370	.lt	LT
Luxembourg	352	.lu	L
Macau	853	.mo	MO
Macedonia	389	.mk	MK
Madagascar	261	.mg	RM
Malawi	265	.mw	MW
Malaysia	60	.my	MAL
Maldives	960	.mv	MV
Mali	223	.ml	RMM
Malta	356	.mt	M
Marshall Is.	692	.mh	MH
Mauritania	222	.mr	RIM
Mauritius	230	.mu	MS
Mexico	52	.mx	MEX
Micronesia	691	.fm	FSM
Moldova	373	.md	MD
Monaco	377	.mc	MC
Mongolia	976	.mn	MGL
Montenegro	382	.me	MNE
Morocco	212	.ma	MA
Mozambique	258	.mz	MOC
Myanmar	95	.mm	BUR
Namibia	264	.na	NAM
Nauru	674	.nr	NAU
Nepal	977	.np	NEP
Netherlands	31	.nl	NL
New Zealand	64	.nz	NZ
Nicaragua	505	.ni	NIC
Niger	227	.ne	RN
Nigeria	234	.ng	WAN
Norway	47	.no	N
Oman	968	.om	OM
Pakistan	92	.pk	PK
Palau	680	.pw	PAL
Palestinian Terr.	970	.ps	PS
Panama	507	.pa	PA
Papua N. Guinea	675	.pg	PNG
Paraguay	595	.py	PY
Peru	51	.pe	PE
Philippines	63	.ph	RP
Poland	48	.pl	PL
Portugal	351	.pt	P
Puerto Rico	1787/1939	.pr	PR
Qatar	974	.qa	Q
Romania	40	.ro	RO
Russian Fed.	7	.ru	RUS
Rwanda	250	.rw	RWA
St. Kitts/Nevis	1869	.kn	SCN
St. Lucia	1758	.lc	WL

Country	Dialling Code	Internet Tld	Plate Code
St. Vincent/Gren.	1784	.vc	WV
Samoa	685	.ws	WS
San Marino	378	.sm	RSM
Sao Tome/Principe	239	.st	STP
Saudi Arabia	966	.sa	SA
Senegal	221	.sn	SN
Serbia	381	.rs	SRB
Seychelles	248	.sc	SY
Sierra Leone	232	.sl	WAL
Singapore	65	.sg	SGP
Slovakia	421	.sk	SK
Slovenia	386	.si	SLO
Solomon Is.	677	.sb	SOL
Somalia	252	.so	SO
South Africa	27	.za	ZA
South Sudan	211	.ss	SSD
Spain	34	.es	E
Sri Lanka	94	.lk	CL
Sudan	249	.sd	SUD
Suriname	597	.sr	SME
Swaziland	268	.sz	SD
Sweden	46	.se	S
Switzerland	41	.ch	CH
Syria	963	.sy	SYR
Taiwan	886	.tw	RC
Tajikistan	992	.tj	TJ
Tanzania	255	.tz	EAT
Thailand	66	.th	T
Timor-Leste	670	.tl	TL
Togo	228	.tg	TG
Tonga	676	.to	TO
Trinidad/Tobago	1868	.tt	TT
Tunisia	216	.tn	TN
Turkey	90	.tr	TR
Turkmenistan	993	.tm	TM
Tuvalu	688	.tv	TUV
Uganda	256	.ug	EAU
Ukraine	380	.ua	UA
Utd. Arab Em.	971	.ae	UAE
Utd. Kingdom	44	.uk	GB
Uruguay	598	.uy	ROU
Usa	1	.us	USA
Uzbekistan	998	.uz	UZ
Vanuatu	678	.vu	VU
Vatican City	39	.va	V
Venezuela	58	.ve	YV
Vietnam	84	.vn	VN
Yemen	967	.ye	YAR
Zambia	260	.zm	RNR
Zimbabwe	263	.zw	ZW

PLACES TO GO

where

when

where

when

-11.00 Samoa

-10.00 Tahiti

-9.00 Anchorage

-8.00 San Francisco

-7.00 Denver

-6.00 Mexico City, Chicago

-5.00 Havana, New York

-4.00 Santiago

-3.00 Buenos Aires, São Paulo

-3.30 Saint John's

-2.00 South Georgia

-1.00 Azores

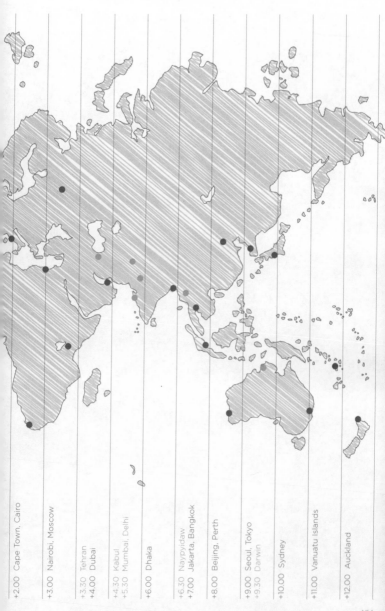

+2.00 Cape Town, Cairo

+3.00 Nairobi, Moscow

+3.30 Tehran
+4.00 Dubai

+4.30 Kabul
+5.30 Mumbai, Delhi

+6.00 Dhaka

+6.30 Naypyidaw
+7.00 Jakarta, Bangkok

+8.00 Beijing, Perth

+9.00 Seoul, Tokyo
+9.30 Darwin

+10.00 Sydney

+11.00 Vanuatu Islands

+12.00 Auckland

ACCEPT NO IMITATIONS · LEGENDARY NOTEBOOKS

INDEX

101

102

103

104

105

106

107

108

109

110

111

112

113

114

115

116

117

118

119

120

121

122

123

124

125

126

127

128

129

130

131

132

133

134

135

136

137

138

139

140

141

142

Blank Pages 143

144

145

146

147

148

149

150

151

152

153

154

155

156

157

158

159

160

PACKING LIST

what I need
what I have
packed

○○○

○○○

○○○

○○○

○○○

○○○

○○○

○○○

○○○

○○○

○○○

○○○

○○○

PACKING LIST

what I need
what I have
packed

○○○

○○○

○○○

○○○

○○○

○○○

○○○

○○○

○○○

○○○

○○○

○○○

○○○

PACKING LIST

what I need
what I have
packed

○○○

○○○

○○○

○○○

○○○

○○○

○○○

○○○

○○○

○○○

○○○

○○○

○○○

○○○

PACKING LIST

what I need
what I have
packed

○○○

○○○

○○○

○○○

○○○

○○○

○○○

○○○

○○○

○○○

○○○

○○○

○○○

○○○

PACKING LIST

what I need
what I have
packed

◯◯◯

◯◯◯

◯◯◯

◯◯◯

◯◯◯

◯◯◯

◯◯◯

◯◯◯

◯◯◯

◯◯◯

◯◯◯

◯◯◯

◯◯◯

PACKING LIST

what I need
what I have
packed

◯◯◯

◯◯◯

◯◯◯

◯◯◯

◯◯◯

◯◯◯

◯◯◯

◯◯◯

◯◯◯

◯◯◯

◯◯◯

◯◯◯

◯◯◯

PACKING LIST

	what I need	what I have	packed
	○	○	○
	○	○	○
	○	○	○
	○	○	○
	○	○	○
	○	○	○
	○	○	○
	○	○	○
	○	○	○
	○	○	○
	○	○	○
	○	○	○
	○	○	○
	○	○	○

PACKING LIST

	what I need	what I have	packed
	○	○	○
	○	○	○
	○	○	○
	○	○	○
	○	○	○
	○	○	○
	○	○	○
	○	○	○
	○	○	○
	○	○	○
	○	○	○
	○	○	○
	○	○	○
	○	○	○

PACKING LIST

	what I need	what I have	packed
	○	○	○
	○	○	○
	○	○	○
	○	○	○
	○	○	○
	○	○	○
	○	○	○
	○	○	○
	○	○	○
	○	○	○
	○	○	○
	○	○	○
	○	○	○

PACKING LIST

	what I need	what I have	packed
	○	○	○
	○	○	○
	○	○	○
	○	○	○
	○	○	○
	○	○	○
	○	○	○
	○	○	○
	○	○	○
	○	○	○
	○	○	○
	○	○	○
	○	○	○

PACKING LIST

what I need
what I have
packed

○○○

○○○

○○○

○○○

○○○

○○○

○○○

○○○

○○○

○○○

○○○

○○○

○○○

PACKING LIST

what I need
what I have
packed

○○○

○○○

○○○

○○○

○○○

○○○

○○○

○○○

○○○

○○○

○○○

○○○

○○○

PACKING LIST

	what I need	what I have packed
	○ ○ ○	
	○ ○ ○	
	○ ○ ○	
	○ ○ ○	
	○ ○ ○	
	○ ○ ○	
	○ ○ ○	
	○ ○ ○	
	○ ○ ○	
	○ ○ ○	
	○ ○ ○	
	○ ○ ○	
	○ ○ ○	

PACKING LIST

	what I need	what I have packed
	○ ○ ○	
	○ ○ ○	
	○ ○ ○	
	○ ○ ○	
	○ ○ ○	
	○ ○ ○	
	○ ○ ○	
	○ ○ ○	
	○ ○ ○	
	○ ○ ○	
	○ ○ ○	
	○ ○ ○	
	○ ○ ○	

PACKING LIST

what I need
what I have
packed

○○○

○○○

○○○

○○○

○○○

○○○

○○○

○○○

○○○

○○○

○○○

○○○

○○○

○○○

PACKING LIST

what I need
what I have
packed

○○○

○○○

○○○

○○○

○○○

○○○

○○○

○○○

○○○

○○○

○○○

○○○

○○○

○○○